IF YOU LOVE READING, THANK
JOHANNES GUTENBERG!

BIOGRAPHY 3RD GRADE

Children's Biography Books

BABY PROFESSOR
EDUCATION KIDS

Speedy Publishing LLC
40 E. Main St. #1156
Newark, DE 19711
www.speedypublishing.com

In this book, we're going to talk about the life of Johannes Gutenberg. So, let's get right to it!

Johannes Gutenberg

WHO WAS
JOHANNES
GUTENBERG?

ohannes Gutenberg was the first European to invent a system of movable type that worked with a printing press. Gutenberg had many talents. He was a blacksmith as well as a goldsmith. He was an inventor and after his invention was up and running, he was a printer and publisher.

He started to experiment with the idea of type that was movable when he was 40 years old. Twelve years later he was able to get an investment from Johann Fust to create his amazing machine, the printing press.

Johannes Gutenberg (right) in engraving from 1881.

Early Life

Gutenberg was born in 1398 in the city of Mainz, Germany. His father was a goldsmith. Little is known about his childhood except that his family moved around the country a few times. While living in Mainz, Gutenberg learned his father's trade. In 1428, many craftsmen were sent into exile from the city, including Gutenberg's family.

Illustration of Johannes Gutenberg.

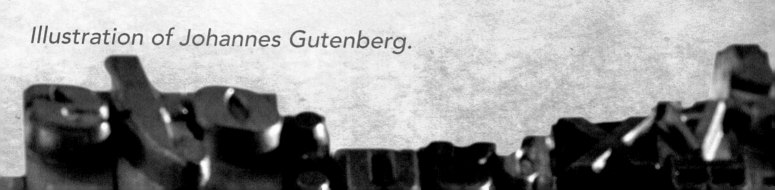

ter, tree ge ... pranius Orne qdqmo prae
up pranius Orne qdqmo prae
ur hoc exprigare.z pfectu ex npfecto hndue

The reason was there had been a rebellion against the wealthy class who were ruling the town. Gutenberg fled to Strasbourg in France where he stayed until 1444.

While living in Strasbourg, Gutenberg began to work on some printing experiments. Up until this time, printing was done with wooden blocks. Gutenberg was well versed in making books already, so he understood the steps involved in making a finished book. He began to make the process of typesetting more flexible.

Johannes Gutenberg.

Johannes Gutenberg Memorial Statue.

His first innovation was movable metal type. He made single letters and characters out of small metal pieces that could be moved and rearranged in different ways. Although a system of movable type with ceramic porcelain pieces had been used in China for centuries, Gutenberg's casting system and the use of alloys of metal made the creation of the type much easier. He also created oil-based inks.

utenberg took existing methods for different types of presses and adapted them to make a machine that could work with his movable type. When he operated his press, he could print thousands of pages per day instead of the standard 40 or so pages per day that was possible with wood block printing. His new machine started a reading revolution.

Printing compositors stick and type case.

Ancient Printing Press.

Prior to this time, only wealthy people owned books because they were so expensive to produce. As the cost of printing books decreased, middle class people could afford them. Gutenberg's machine became popular across Europe very quickly. Books were printed at a pace they had never been created before.

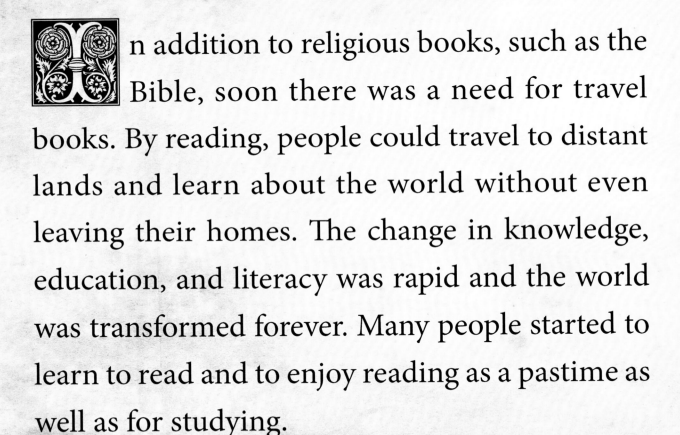

In addition to religious books, such as the Bible, soon there was a need for travel books. By reading, people could travel to distant lands and learn about the world without even leaving their homes. The change in knowledge, education, and literacy was rapid and the world was transformed forever. Many people started to learn to read and to enjoy reading as a pastime as well as for studying.

William Caxton showing specimens of his printing to King Edward IV and his Queen.

Printing Press, 1520.

There was a chance for the ordinary person to obtain knowledge through the wonders of reading. It was as if someone had turned a light on in a dark room. Gutenberg's invention had started a transformation in society that eventually helped bring about the Scientific Revolution as well as the blossoming of art and culture during the High Renaissance period.

Printing Press Tools

Which Were The First Books Printed By Gutenberg?

Historians believe that the first printed sheet from the Gutenberg press was a poem written in German. Other printed materials were books for learning Latin grammar as well as indulgences used by the Catholic Church. These indulgences were issued to people so they wouldn't spend too much time in purgatory after they died.

The Gutenberg Bible.

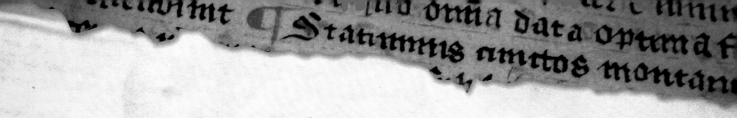

However, Gutenberg's masterpiece was his Bible. It was the first time that a Bible had been produced by machine. They had always been painstakingly transcribed by hand. For the first time, the Bible was available to individuals who were not clergymen. Prior to Gutenberg's time, Bibles were very rare. It might take a monk an entire year to transcribe a Bible by hand.

Ancient Texts.

The **_Gutenberg Bible_** was written in Latin and had two columns on most pages with 42 lines of type. Most of the Bibles he created had 1,286 pages. They were so big that they had to be bound in two different volumes. Gutenberg only printed 180 of these Bibles, but they were amazing books. Only 49 copies have survived to today and many of them have missing pages.

Gutenberg Bible (Pelplin copy).

Incipit prologus sancti iheronimi presbiteri i parabolas salomonis ☙ Iungat epistola quos iūgit saerdotiū: immo carta non diuidat: quos xpi nectit amor. Cōmentarios in osee. amos. z zachariā malachiā quoqȝ pscēas. scripsisse: si licuisset pre valitudine. Mittitis solacia sumptuum notarios nros et librarios sustentans: ut vobis poīssimū nrm desudet ingeniū. Et ecce ex latere frequens turba diuisa poscitū: quasi aut equū sit me vobis esurientibȝ alijs laborare: aut in ratione dati et accepti cuiusȝ preter vos obnoxius sim. Itaqȝ lōga egrotatione fractus. ne penitus hoc anno reticerem: z apud vos mutus essem. vidui opus nomini vro consecraui. interptatione videlicet triū salomonis voluminū: masloth qd hebrei pabolas. vulgata editio pūbia vocat: coeleth. que grece ecclesiasten. latine cōcionatorem possumus dicere: sirasirim. qd ī linguā nram vertit canticū cāticorū. Fertur et panaretos. iesu filij sirach liber: z alius pseudographus. qui sapientia salomonis inscribitur. Quos priore hebraicum repperi. nō ecclesiasticū ut apud latinos: sed pabolas pnotatū. Cui iūcti erant ecclesiastes. et canticū canticorū: ut similitudinē salomonis. nō solū numero librorū: sed etiā materiaȝ genere coequaret. Secūdus apud hebreos nusȝ est: quia et ipse stilus grecam eloquentiā redolet: et nōnulli scriptorū veteres hunc esse iudei filonis affirmāt. Sicut ergo iudith z thobie z machabeorū libros. legit quidē eos ecclesia. sed inter canonicas scripturas nō recipit: sic z hec duo volumina legat ad edificatione plebis: nō ad auctoritatem ecclesiasticorū dogmatū affirmandam.

Si cui sane septuaginta interpretum magis editio placet: habet eā a nobis olim emedatā. Neqȝ enim nova sic cudimus: ut vetera destruam. Et tamē cū diligentissime legerit: sciat magis nra scripta intelligi: que nō in tertiū vas translusa coacuerit: sed statim de prelo purissime emedata teste: suū saporē seruauerit. Incipiūt parabole salomois.

Parabole salomonis filij dauid regis irl: ad sciendā sapientiā z disciplinā: ad intelligenda verba prudentie et suscipienda eruditionē doctrine: iustitiā et iudiciū z equitatē: ut detur paruulis astutia: et adolescenti scientia et intellectus. Audiens sapiens sapientior erit: z intelliges gubernacula possidebit. Animaduertet parabolam et interpretationem: verba sapientiū z enigmata eorū. Timor dūi principiū sapientie. Sapientiam atqȝ doctrinam stulti despiciūt. Audi fili mi disciplinā pris tui et ne dimittas legem mris tue: ut addatur gracia capiti tuo: z torques collo tuo. Fili mi si te lactauerint peccatores: ne acquiescas eis. Si dixerint veni nobiscū insidiemur sanguini: abscondam insidias cōtra insontem frustra: deglutiamus eū sicut infernus viuentem z integrum quasi descendentem in lacū: omnem preciosam substantiā reperiemus: implebimus domus nras spolijs. sortem mitte nobiscum. marsupiū sit unum omniū nrm: fili mi ne ambules cū eis. Prohibe pedem tuū a semitis eorū. Pedes enim illorū ad malū currūt: z festināt ut effundant sāguinem. Frustra autem iacitur rete ante oculos pēnatorū. Ipsi quoqȝ cōtra sanguinē suū insidiantur: et

It's estimated that if a complete copy were to be auctioned today it would be purchased for $35 million dollars or more. Unfortunately, despite the fact that in his day the Bibles were each sold for a large sum, 30 gold coins named florins, Gutenberg never made much money from his work.

Gutenberg's Financial Troubles

Gutenberg invented the printing press in 1444 AD. In 1448, he left Strasbourg and returned to Mainz. Two years later he had set up his own print shop. He had borrowed a large amount of money from an investor by the name of Johann Fust so he could set up his business. Gutenberg needed the money to create his unique movable type and printing presses.

Johann Fust (1400-1466).

Printer in 1568.

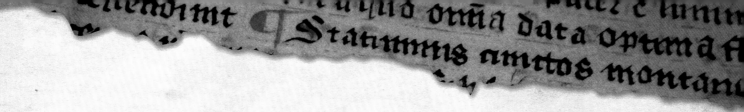

By 1452 Gutenberg was in debt and he couldn't pay Fust back. A new agreement was put into place so that Fust would be a full partner in Gutenberg's printing business.

Peter Schoeffer, who was Fust's son-in-law, joined the project and historians believe that he and Gutenberg set up two presses to print the 42-line Gutenberg Bible. Schoeffer became Gutenberg's apprentice. It's believed that Schoeffer created some of the first typefaces, which are different styles and designs of type.

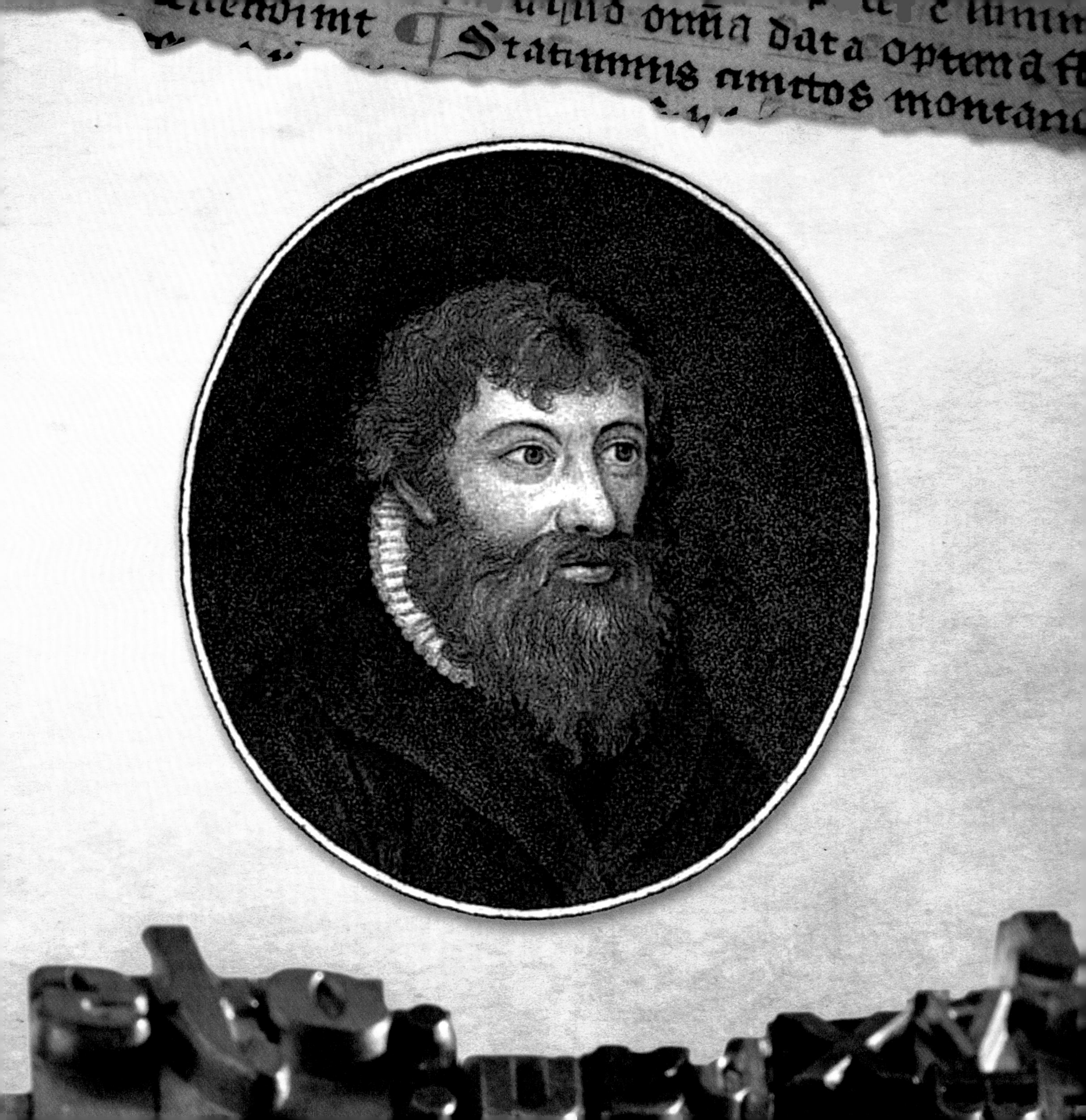
omīa data optima
Statuimus amicos

Gutenberg Bible.

In 1455, the business was making money from the indulgences the Church was having printed and also from the Bibles, but Gutenberg was still in debt. Fust had invested 1,600 florins in the business and the debt was now a huge 20,000 florins. Fust sued Gutenberg and Gutenberg lost the lawsuit. Fust now gained control over the print shop and half of Gutenberg's beautifully printed Bibles belonged to Fust.

ust and Schoeffer published the first book that included the printer's name and date. It was the *Mainz Psalter,* which was a book of psalms. It was the second book that had been printed with movable type. Printed books were available in August of 1457 and Fust and Schoeffer proudly stated how the books were produced, but they made no mention of the inventor of their presses—Gutenberg.

Mainz Psalter: Johann Fust & Peter Schoeffer (printers).

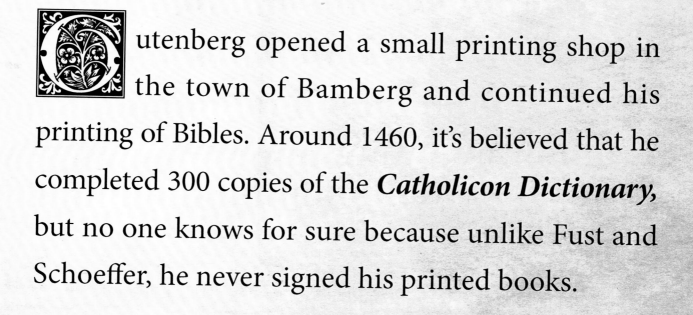

Detail of a Letterpress.

utenberg opened a small printing shop in the town of Bamberg and continued his printing of Bibles. Around 1460, it's believed that he completed 300 copies of the **Catholicon Dictionary,** but no one knows for sure because unlike Fust and Schoeffer, he never signed his printed books.

n 1462, there was a warlike conflict in Mainz called the Mainz Diocesan Feud. Many people in the town were killed as the town was plundered and Gutenberg fled. Archbishop Adolp Von Nassau took over the rule of the diocese. Gutenberg settled in the city of Eltville and managed a small press that he didn't own. Von Nassau changed his mind and asked Gutenberg to come back to Mainz in 1465.

Replica of the Gutenberg press at the International Printing Museum in Carson, California.

Typography workshop. Old metallic letters for printing with old book.

Von Nassau gave Gutenberg an official title of Gentleman of the Court and approved a monthly salary for him as well as allotments of grain and wine. Gutenberg passed away in 1468 AD at the age of 70. Sadly, his contributions were not known worldwide at the time of his death.

Gutenberg Museum in Mainz, Germany.

GUTENBERG'S LEGACY

lthough Gutenberg never became wealthy from his inventions or businesses, he changed the world. If it hadn't been for the printing press, many people would never have had the opportunity to own books of their own. If you love reading, the world becomes open to you, and it's as easy as opening the pages in a book.

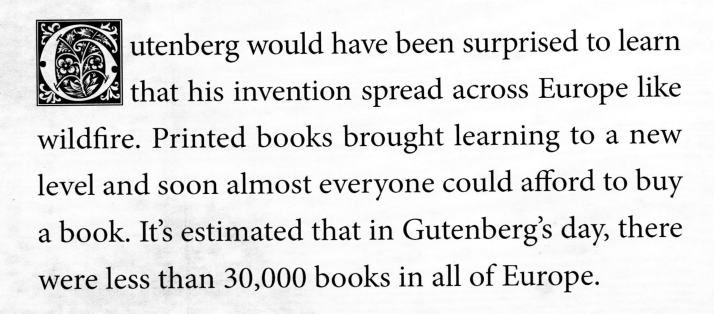

Gutenberg would have been surprised to learn that his invention spread across Europe like wildfire. Printed books brought learning to a new level and soon almost everyone could afford to buy a book. It's estimated that in Gutenberg's day, there were less than 30,000 books in all of Europe.

Metal Letterpress Types.

Within just a few decades, the printing press spread to over a dozen European countries and more than two hundred towns and cities. By the year 1500, the printing businesses in Europe had printed more than 20 million books. From the years 1501 to 1600, the output of books increased by a factor of 10 and there were 200 million books in print.

Old metallic letters for printing.

Old typography printing machine.

The oldest digital library in the world was created in 1971. It's a vast storehouse of books that are now available that can be read on the computer and on tablets. It was called Project Gutenberg to honor Johannes Gutenberg, the man who started the reading revolution.

Vienna, Austria: City landscape with Johannes Gutenberg memorial.

 wesome! Now you know more about Johannes Gutenberg and the legacy of his invention, the printing press. You can find more Biography books from Baby Professor by searching the website of your favorite book retailer.

Visit

BABY PROFESSOR
EDUCATION KIDS

www.BabyProfessorBooks.com

to download Free Baby Professor eBooks
and view our catalog of new and exciting
Children's Books

51056323R00038

Made in the USA
San Bernardino, CA
29 August 2019